The Relationship Playbook for Women

7 Questions for you and your soulmate

YVETTE WEIR

The Relationship Playbook for Women:
7 Questions for you and your soulmate
Copyright ©2021 by Yvette Weir

Contents

Introduction 1
Chapter 1: Who am I? 5
Chapter 2: Is he Emotionally Available? 11
Chapter 3: Does he have the three C's? 17
Chapter 4: Is he a Macy or Marshall's Shopper? 23
Chapter 5: What's in this for me? 29
Chapter 6: Are You Healthy? 35
Chapter 7: Would you do it again? 41
Chapter 8: The God Who Answers Questions .45
Chapter 9: Communication Cheat Sheets 49
    Ten Phrases to Practice out loud with Confidence . 49
    Seven Key Questions to Remember 50
    Five Affirmations to get you started each day 50
Epilogue 51

DEDICATION

The Relationship Playbook is dedicated to the memory of my late brother Trevor Weir, who was a fine writer and lover of language and prose as well as an avid sportsman and computer specialist. He encouraged me to write with original and meticulous detail. His inspiration lives on as I paint with words a vivid picture of my experience.

Trevor and I grew up with a love for reading and you would rarely see us at home or in public without a book in our backpack or in the car. Although he never officially published in this manner, he wrote volumes of emails, texts and courses - professionally and personally. I would start up a "What do you think about this , topic - Trevor?" And he would run with it on email, sometimes we included other family members in our private writing 'dumps.' There was literally no topic I could suggest that ever stumped him! His incredible and powerful mind gave him the ability to not only weigh in verbally but to write his thoughts eloquently and with credibility.

He has passed on his love of prose to his children, several of whom are also writers.

This book is dedicated to the children of the Weir and Brown family - may all their relationships be healthy and strong because they were brave enough to ask questions.

ACKNOWLEDGEMENTS

Every book comes to life with a team. If I did not have my team "WRITE THAT BOOK" you would not have this book in your hand today. They never stopped gently and insistently asking for its whereabouts. They treated it like I had misplaced it somewhere in my house and I needed to bring it out because the company was stopping by. To my early encouragers, Jaymie Pottinger, Howard Bailey, Jet, Gabrielle, and Joel Gladstone, thank you for never letting me rest. My readers - love you all so much, you listened so patiently and gave me feedback and momentum to keep going. Ray Nelson is a friend who I called endlessly to listen to "Just one more chapter, real quick!" My editor helped polish and shine my initial manuscript. Thank you so much.

If I have left out any name from the team "WRITE THAT BOOK" my apologies, know that every suggestion, encouragement, and endorsement has been greatly appreciated in the creation of **The Relationship Playbook.** *My Greatest thanks to my Heavenly Father from whom originates every great and perfect gift - including writing - may He always be honored and glorified in all that I do.*

Introduction

I never knew that dedicating twenty-one years of my life to one individual would end in failure and a sense of nothingness. In the aftermath of a court event, my Ex escorted me to my car and then asked if I wanted to pray. At least that's what I thought it sounded like because in my mind I was saying, "Are you serious?" The sense of misplaced piety would merge into indifference as the years rolled on. Mostly, I was made to feel as if I had only been a surrogate for his children.

No one can make you feel any more than what you allow them to, right? That's not the easiest question to answer. I dare you to respond only if you have walked a mile in my moccasins, listened to my story, or have known someone with a similar profile.

My Ex came very close on his own to making me feel worthless, useless, and incompetent. When did these lies begin? Where was his conscience, emotions, or sense of justice during or after? These are mostly rhetorical questions. No one really knows him, not even his closest family members. You can't really know anyone who won't let you in. I spent years around him and in the end, I know his behavioral patterns, his tendencies, and biases, but not the true man. Our emotional relationship stayed on the surface.

I didn't win. But I can learn.

That life lesson was costly. I was innocent, naive, and didn't ask the right questions. **The Relationship Playbook for Women** is written straightforwardly with questions that start from the very beginning of the romantic relationship to the end, if it unfortunately goes there. Don't miss a single question on this journey, and make sure to check out the Communication Cheatsheet Chapter which will be a quick reference guide moving forward.

During my marriage, it only took a few questions on pertinent sticky matters to realize I would be shut down because he did not care to respond or my questions were deemed unnecessary. Instead of persisting, I gave up and there were sinkholes of information we should have shared and processed jointly that got lost. I was no longer transparent and open, everything was filtered through his privacy code. We did not have joint friends or hang out with other married folk or family, it would have called for too much of an emotional investment for him.

I had no sister mentor, guide, or playbook. I did not know what to ask at the beginning of the relationship or towards the end.

I know now.

I am on a journey of healing and restoration. There are days and encounters when the emotional sting of the past can rear its ugly head and I go through the day just silently shaking my head. Most other days I find myself rejoicing that I am free and able to conduct my life as I please. It can take years to regain your stride.

Be kind and gentle with yourself.
Love the person you are becoming or rediscovering.
This is my story. Before and after.
It is my gift to you - start asking questions.
See you in Chapter One

Chapter 1

Who am I?

*"When a woman becomes her own best friend life is easier." - **Diane Von Furstenberg***

I met my Ex at church one Sabbath. The best place to meet a significant other, right? Shared faith. Shared lifestyles. Shared goals. Maybe? Each person still needs to be vetted with questions. This is the reason for dating with a purpose - discovery.

He was ten years older, much more conservative on many fronts but very attentive. Watch the **attention.** It is seductive to have our phones ring three nights consecutively with a deep baritone voice at the other end. Especially after it's been silent for months! We take leave of our senses in the euphoria of emotional attention.

My Ex handed me a 'blank check' one night as we stood on my balcony overlooking the parking lot with a full moon in front of us and a gentle breeze behind while he asked, "What are you looking for in a man?" I looked back at him like a deer caught in the headlights, blinded by the simplicity of the question because I did not know. He had a penetrating way of cocking his head to the side and looking deep into your soul as if you were the only one that mattered in the Universe. I giggled nervously and responded with some kind of nonsense to fill in the silence. I hadn't taken the time to really examine myself and the core values that were important to me, much less realizing my purpose in life. So I could not answer that question.

Without knowing yourself, you can NEVER know who will be a complementary match or soulmate. You can sense passion. You know how they make you feel. You can line up the data like, cultural backgrounds, education, and faith, but it pales in comparison to honestly knowing **yourself** and the type of person that will best fit the unique gifts God has given you.

I am a person of much fun and laughter. My brother and I used to have long conversations that were punctuated by such belly-roaring laughter you would be crying with hilarity. He taught me how to live outside of the box and acting just a 'little bit crazy' half the time was a part of our DNA.

My parents were always entertaining and I grew up in a household that had extended family and guests passing through all the time. My parents also traveled frequently for work, so travel was a normal part of my life.

Did he come into my life and understand my hardwiring? My Ex understood the rhythm of travel, you might say we perfected that, but in other crucial aspects nurtured by my family dynamics, we were opposites.

In the challenging years following the marriage, I would often reflect on that simple question he asked that would have given me a perfect opportunity to express my core values. But I didn't know myself and my answer was superficial and basic - enough to satisfy him so that he could fulfill that which I didn't even know how to articulate.

The flip side of this question - Who am I? Who are you? My family forged a part of my identity and behavior that is embedded in me. I have raised my children in a way that I know is similar to my own upbringing. I fought for christian education for them because most of my family education included private school. I still hear the fact that his siblings' children all did public school and turned out just fine. My mother sent me on bus, taxi and train wherever we lived to make sure that I stayed in Christian schools from the time I was ten years old! These are discussions and compromises that should be discussed ahead of time.

What are his behavioral patterns? Did his mom stay at home or did she work? (that will largely shape his expectation of you). What kind of crazies did he have going on in his family (we all have skeletons in the family closet)? How was he raised, absent father or both parents? Wealthy or humble beginnings? What are his thoughts on diversity, especially if living in the US or Canada? Due to the times we are living in I would also include his thoughts on Vaccination , which seems to follow one's family background as well as the

CDC guidelines. Gently probing, is similar to going deep in the relationship at the cellular level of what really influenced your significant other's upbringing which can linger well into adulthood. I knew but a drop in the proverbial cup of any of these questions before and even while I was married.

Why? I didn't know the importance of dating for a purpose. A purpose that would illuminate or confirm our compatibility for each other and a person's background sets the stage for his present thinking and mindset. We don't have to be carbon copy of the past, especially if it were negative, but there may be lingering unresolved issues that you should listen out for. My parents grew up in the same small town and were actually distant relatives. The Weirs and the Johnsons knew each other well. That will rarely happen in today's world of global mobility and second and third relationships and marriages.

Guy Francois, in his book **"The Adversity Success Principles"** speaks courageously about his Haitian past and the secrets kept like elephants in the room. Only by confronting the forbidden skeletons was he able to move on and lead a successful life. So if a man does not or will not with time, open up and share from his past, that's a huge red flag! And we can't always find or interview his old family or friends, who will only give the polished version. anyway. You want a man who will bravely tell it like it was!

There is no judgment on the decisions of our childhood. Adults in our lives made these calls for us and we lived through them. To not share is to be ashamed or too scarred by our formative years and either choice is an unhealthy beginning to a new relationship. But what did my 25-year-old self know?

Every lady should spend some time alone intentionally before a relationship begins or right after a serious one has ended. I spent a considerable amount of years in school studying for a terminal degree and then precious little time alone before the relationship began. We need to do some serious introspection with ourselves and fall head over heels in love with the person that God has created. Our personalities are a unique blend of our cultures, environment, upbringing, and even our imaginations! We need time in our young adult years to explore and get comfortable with ourselves and our own company. There will be relationships that form from undergrad and that run at breakneck speed into a long and permanent union and others like mine that are short and swift but I would still take deliberate and measured time to enjoy, understand and date you.

Take a gap year post-college. Live alone. Manage your own finances.Venture out. Be self-sufficient. Save some money. Invest some money. Give away some money. Embrace the silence. Learn new interests. Love on you.

Digging Deeper -

Set aside some quiet time to think about what matters most to you, the things and activities that are important to you on a daily, weekly and monthly basis. How does your faith guide these actions and lifestyles? Write three core values then use the above to craft a mission statement for your life and the kind of person that would be the most compatible to join you.

My Mission Statement

_____

_____

_____

_____

_____

_____

_____

_____

_____

_____

_____

_____

_____

_____

_____

_____

_____

_____

_____

_____

_____

_____

_____

Chapter 2

Is he Emotionally Available?

*Should your fountains be dispersed abroad, Streams of water in the streets? - **Proverbs 5:16***

You have put the work in and you know yourself. Your likes based on your experiences and how you are hardwired. You think you've found a compatible soulmate. But is he ready? This question encompasses emotional readiness and intimacy. "In-to-me-you see." If you say those words quickly it literally describes the word - intimacy. A person who is willing to let you see inside or beyond the facades that we share with the public and is making himself emotionally available for true intimacy.

Matthew Kelly in his book, ***"The Seven Levels of Intimacy,"*** also describes intimacy this way,

It is the process of mutual self-revelation that inspires us to give ourselves completely to another person in the mystery wevcall love.

11

Let's explore what it means for him to be emotionally available and ready for intimacy.

Can you be involved, dating and going down the aisle and not be sure if he is emotionally ready?

Absolutely!

Because a man (and woman) may confuse physical readiness or sex for emotional readiness.

Because it takes less effort to get physically naked than emotionally naked (not that I'm promoting the former before marriage mind you).

Because becoming emotionally available means transparency, vulnerability, and getting uncomfortable and not everyone is willing to go there as much as crave the thought of intimacy.

A good friend started dating after years of a 'drought' season. She found a man who is attentive to her every desire. Not just giving **attention.**

There is a subtle, but important nuance to both words.

One gives time and heart and the latter only time.

She describes him with joy and laughter in her voice. So infectious! I am rooting for them so hard, even though I have never met him, because of how he makes her feel - like a queen. Because her emotional and physical needs are already being met and her love bucket is overflowing! She has wisely realized that there are more important elements than just looks in a relationship and I anticipate hearing about wedding bells soon.

Watch for these signs of a healthy man who is emotionally vulnerable and in love.

He tells stories from his past. Whether good, bad, or ugly, he's a person with a past (as is everyone for that matter) and he's not afraid to share it. I've heard such amazing and deep stories in my dating years, but rarely did my Ex share his stories.

He involves you with his family. Traditionally, men have gone to visit the family when they are close to an engagement level or even to formally ask a father for his daughter's hand in marriage as did mine). But a great sign of his emotional commitment is his willingness to involve you *early* in his most primary relationship - family. You should hang out and spend time getting to know the family that might one day be yours also. His introduction to the family signals the bond that he hopes you will build with them as well as himself. My bond was very loose to non-existent at times with his family. We did not spend quality and early time getting to know each other and they even openly questioned my parenting skills.

He goes public. I get it, that he might not be a Facebook kind of man and may claim to value his privacy, but he is nevertheless unashamed to declare you his number one love in other public ways. You might worship together or volunteer together. When he thinks it appropriate you might do things together as a family in public if he has children. He will not keep you as the 'best-kept secret' from the world. PDA (public displays of affection) is a natural part of his expression of love.

He misses you when you are not around. He might demonstrate that by keeping in touch via phone or text or even an old-fashioned card. A man who is making himself emotionally available to you will want to stay in touch and keep you in the loop.

He communicates. Women love talkers, dreamers, visionaries and it all comes in via strong communication. He speaks in the future tense with you. He favors the inclusive 'we' and 'us' pronoun over 'you' and 'me.' He is willing to learn your love language and time flies when you're together. He values your opinion and incorporates your advice where appropriate.

He prioritizes non-sexual attention and affection. Sex is not intimacy. Say that again a couple of times in your mind. It is a part of intimacy and could be considered the dessert. Do we eat dessert for sustenance? No. Many men have been taking off clothes and becoming physically naked as a matter of course in their relationships, but how many are peeling back the onion layers of who they really are? I placed it near last because if he has made it through the first five, he is in such a good place that his affection and sense of control should be on point. He has so many other tools in his toolbox to express and declare his emotional availability that can supersede his desire to just be physical. Notwithstanding, his affection might be expressed by tender touches and a desire to be physically close without crossing that invisible boundary that sends you over the edge.

Finally, a man who can allow God to show him how to be vulnerable, possess sexual control and still be strong in a relationship with emotional openness is a man who will inspire love and a sense of security in you.

He wants to cultivate the best version of you.

Digging Deeper - Journal or reflect on what that would mean for you?

Chapter 3

Does he have the three C's?

Without Commitment nothing happens —**TD Jakes**

You want to assess whether or not he has the three C's. They blossom at different times, but ultimately, you can not have a lasting relationship without each of them. The first is chemistry, the second compatibility, and the final commitment. Some cultures are heavy on commitment and such relationships may move into marriage and last. In the West, we fall in love differently and the other two are equally as important.

I like how one person described chemistry - that something about a person that draws you in. Often that 'something' is physical and we have family, societal and cultural clues that guide us into who we think fits the bill with chemistry and beauty.

I come from a family of fairly tall men. It would be fair to say that I am drawn to taller men - first, although not exclusively. The men in my family mostly did not wear beards. They either didn't tend to be hairy or shaved facial hair off religiously. I am not particularly drawn to men with a lot of facial hair either, especially if it is long enough to be braided! But on the contrary, thicker eyebrows were rare in my family tribe and perhaps that's one feature that caught me with my Ex and that I still think is downright sexy and intriguing. Oh, the places and expressions I would see with a thicker brow!

We typically magnify the physical in our definition of chemistry or beauty and the more points we can measure the better. A high school crush of mine had multiple points I could measure that lent weight to his sex appeal, aka chemistry. He was tall and well built at seventeen, with thick eyebrows (that's probably where it all began), and an overall goodlooking face. His occasional glance my way seemed to look right through my awkward self.

But what drew me more than his physical appeal was a sense of confidence. Maybe his family had money (I am not sure) and his good looks had always attracted a fan club. I know this was a huge part of his attraction and chemistry. Unfortunately, this feeling was not mutual and I remained an ordinary classmate in his mind. Just to underscore how fleeting good looks can be, I saw a rare picture of him on Facebook after more than thirty years. He looked wasted and weathered as if life had not been kind to him at all!

I have assessed chemistry as I have gotten older and I place more emphasis on inner qualities than my younger self would ever have done. There is chemistry for me when I meet an alpha male who is confident, tall (that's the icing on the cake) with thick eyebrows, and demonstrated leadership. I am also drawn to kindness and a Godly man. You have to be realistic and honest with what chemistry really means to you and what your parameters are. Although chemistry causes you to lean into potential mates, don't build your relationship on chemistry, it only gets the fire started. The wood and substance that will cause your fire to be sustainable at whatever level is compatibility.

I didn't think we were compatible. I thought my Ex was too conservative in dress and behavior. I was young and forever 21. I still am and with the passing of time, my youthful energy and interests were not matched.

I did not know about compatibility as a question to assess with him or to really take stock of what might have been common interests. Much of the dating and courting took place while I lived in Cameroon for a year.

What I could say then was that he showered me with attention.

There is a popular quote on the internet that states, "It's not so much how compatible you are, but how you deal with incompatibility." I would beg to differ, although it might be a matter of semantics. I want to be in a relationship that clearly celebrates that which we have in common and the few things that we don't - I will decide if I can live with. I am an outdoorsy person and camping, skiing and backpacking would be right up my alley. I begged my Ex for years to go camping with me or to go with the church youth groups when they went out. It was not his thing and some of it came from cultural and upbringing experiences. And I missed that window to share all about my outdoor proclivities!

Somewhere around year six or seven, I asked on a few occasions, "What can we do with each other, we have to find something?" I sensed we were moving away from each other.

We lacked the fun and meaningful activities that could have bonded us. We found each other in church, but we didn't have ministries together - in or outside of the church (now he is a regular street evangelist). I went on mission trips solo, I started an informal faith-based group at my office alone. We didn't have any sports in common and even walking together as a couple was infrequent. This was an early sign of a breakdown in the relationship.

The third C stands for commitment. When the fire is dying, is he committed to attending to it? Scrambling to find more wood or fluid or will he stand by and watch it fizzle? How can you assess this quality before you get in?

Ask questions on past situations and see how he handled them. Is he quick to give up? Does he appear stable in the jobs, homes, or relationships he has had in the past? Role-play situations and scenarios that a couple might encounter and see if his answers are satisfactory to you.

Also while he may have the ability to stay committed to a relationship, what is the quality of that relationship? I have seen too many couples who stay together for convenience and ease rather than true love and commitment. Try not to become one of the "married-but-living single" folk.

Questions to ponder as you examine compatibility:

If you had to spend significant time in the same place without work or children as a distraction, would you be comfortable with each other?

What three or more activities or hobbies do you enjoy in common?

Do you like volunteering together?

Is he a cultural or a sports fan? Do you like to eat out or do you cook together?

Does he have an unusual interest or activity that he can spend time teaching or sharing with you?

Does he like or would he support your number one passion or interest?

Do you enjoy worshiping and sharing spiritual truths?

Chemistry, compatibility, and commitment go hand in hand in the best relationships. Know the difference and importance of each.

Digging Deeper - Feel free to add to this list, but this should give you an idea of the direction of your thoughts and questions as you contemplate bringing him into your life.

Chapter 4

Is he a Macy or Marshall's Shopper?

You aren't wealthy until you have something money can't buy. —**Garth Brooks**

What do these two have in common? They both start with the same letter, they are national brands, they sell similar items for clothing and the household. But if you look closely they are very different.

Men can look and act charming and play the perfect gentleman until you broach the subject of money. We did not have decent, sustained, or intelligent discussions about money - ever. Money in a relationship like in business can be used as a power tool.

What a tragedy!

The top three reasons for divorce in America include basic incompatibility (43%), infidelity (28%), and money issues (22%), according to a 2013 study of certified divorce financial analysts.

"I have long believed financial disagreements to be the most common cause of marital conflict and ultimately divorce," says Justin A. Reckers, a CDFA professional based in San Diego, CA. "Now we have empirical evidence proving this is the case across all socio-economic classes." Disparate goals and values around money, coupled with the power and control financial prosperity represent makes money a common battleground in marriages, Reckers adds.

I am not surprised in hindsight that I fell right into the 'disparate goals and values' pit with my Ex. First of all, without prior conversations on money management and goals, we operated more as roommates in this regard. You make your money and do this with it, and I make my money and do that with it. We had separate bank accounts for most if not all of the marriage. I never saw what he made, what funds came through his hands, or the challenges or planning that went into the semi lavish lifestyle of the early part of our marriage.

Why??

Early on it was tacitly agreed by him - 'Don't ask, so I won't have to tell.' When I got insistent he brushed me off like an annoying fly, so I stopped inquiring. His claim to fame in the marriage was providing expensive cars in the relationship and living (especially in the beginning) in the best neighborhoods possible. One day I picked up the book, "The Millionaire Next Door." It was an eye-opener. We lived like millionaires, but we didn't act like them. He was so offended when I pointed that detail out.

We went to a church financial seminar once. That was a one-and-done deal for him. I want to feel that the more he kept me ignorant and unaware of our true financial picture, or my understanding about finances, the more control (and sometimes damage) could be had in the relationship. It was a strong factor in the demise of our relationship along with incompatibility. The lack of financial compatibility and openness destroyed any chance of a relationship and its effects lingered with devastating tenacity years after the marriage ended.

We can not be shy about asking for and demanding financial accountability. To demand means there's a cover. If a relationship is healthy and transparent, demanding accountability can be replaced with sharing the financial state, like sharing and planning for the future or discussing about kids. A dishonest man will cover his tracks even while appearing to display wealth in your face and provide expensive gifts on occasion. It is NOT enough.

Financial conversations like sexual conversations are the hardest and most uncomfortable to address in a relationship. We have to normalize it before we get too involved. If you are a couple in your twenties you are having a slightly different conversation because you are in the building stage of life. You are entering your careers, laying your foundation, and dealing with student loans. Your questions will be different.

In the middle years of life, it is even more important to know how he spent his first twenty years financially and what his goals are for the future, specifically retirement and charitable giving.

You want to gauge how transparent he is in this arena. What is his body language or inclination to be open with these kinds of discussions? Obviously, if you just met the chap you are not delving deep into his personal business, but you can watch attitudes and learn a lot about his generosity towards giving and helping others then assess if it aligns with your financial philosophy. Could be that he is more open and generous than you are and that also would not bode well for compatibility in this area. When the relationship gets more serious your questions should be more specific. This is an extremely important arena to probe.

Five Questions in the beginning:

1. How did your parents handle money and finances when you were growing up?

2. Did they share financial responsibility or was one treated as the 'expert?'

3. How did they use credit cards back then, what are your thoughts on credit and credit card usage now?

4. If you won the lottery or received an unexpected inheritance - how would you spend it?

5. Do you believe in tithing and giving offerings to the church?

Five Questions when the relationship is serious:

1. What are your thoughts on a working mom versus a stay at home mom?

2. What are your thoughts on a prenuptial agreement (relevant with established couples)?

3. How will we combine our households, will we purchase a new home and what about pre-existing debts?

4. What is your risk level with investments?

5. If we have young adult children in the relationship what are his thoughts on sharing any assets before, during (or on the death of a spouse)?

There are SO many questions that can shape and determine attitudes and the direction of a relationship. The root of money and finances is trust and a desire to make the other person happy and secure as you work as partners in the relationship. If you are a Christian your views on money and its relevance in the grand scheme and big picture of life will be different from the one who is not. Someone might want to live more simply and be more philanthropic in their outlook and practice. The other party might see beautiful things of the world as something to acquire and is more dialed into a luxury lifestyle. Is it possible to have both? You will never know if you don't have these conversations and ask questions.

He was both a Marshall's and a Macy shopper. When he wanted to go simple and basic I was allowed to walk the aisles with him and view his purchases. When he privately toggled over to Macy's, I was nowhere near him nor aware of expensive purchases in the thousands that went right over my innocent head.

There is a secular minded tendency with older couples to not marry and instead maintain long standing relationships. This is supposedly to keep finances separate with pensions, benefits and 401K nice and tidy for respective households and adult children. Don't let that be your high barrier to living as man and wife someday. Have the hard and difficult conversations early and decide on an action plan that will work for you.

Digging Deeper - What other areas can you include in this financial discussion? Make sure you journal these after some self reflection. Everyone's financial situation is unique ranging from large amounts of debt or bankruptcy to none of the former, but little savings and investments. What will you be comfortable with and how will you merge your households?

Chapter 5

What's in this for me?

A good name is to be chosen rather than great riches, loving favor rather than silver and gold —**Proverbs 22:1**

The first four questions were regarding an intact relationship. A hopeful one is like a treasure chest full of laces and dreams, love songs, and candlelit dinners. Dancing by the moonlight, sharing soft kisses, you walked around starry-eyed with his picture as your screensaver.

But you didn't ask enough questions or you hadn't found this book on time to guide you.

I am so sorry.

This chapter is crucial. It will save you from financial heartache and remorse. It is also the shortest chapter because I am going to refer you out for professional help. I am clearly not the expert and fell tremendously in this area. I had always hoped we could be the poster couple for how with God all things are possible. But you have to be willing to WORK and when that stops and commitment is not a staple of the relationship - *It's over.*

At the time that you unilaterally or mutually agree that for whatever reason the honeymoon is permanently over - and I am not here to judge or cajole you out of a decision, I am here for support - you must ask yourself this question, " What's in this for me?"

Realize two things. You knew how to be married or you learned it on the job and you don't know how to be divorced or the steps that are involved, unless you've gone through it before. Marriage is ideally an unselfish covenant between two lovers. A time and place where you both mutually look out for and safeguard each other's happiness via love and commitment. Divorce is the exact opposite. You have to assume he is going to look out for himself, therefore you need to do likewise.

Unless you are a lawyer, let's leave the process to the experts. We got married and the pastor facilitated the process. Even though it is possible to have an uncontested or even DIY online divorce, that is the most foolish thing!

Always use an attorney.

Do not leave and accept mementos like a few pieces of furniture and allow him to keep what really matters: the real estate, pension, 401 K, and other tangible assets you are entitled to splitting. The timeshare, boat, car or RV - you get the picture. A professional will also help you navigate and uncover other aspects you might not have thought about over the years or weren't privy to knowing.

Without clearcut legal protection, anything and everything is up for grabs. You won't know down the line who is responsible for what. And don't sign anything once this path has begun without first consulting an attorney.

It's not being mean or getting even. It's acting with wisdom and prudence and securing your future. The longer you are married the more important it is to be mindful when deconstructing the building.

You will need as many of the blocks as possible to begin again.

Our marriage could have been represented as a building that was ten stories high.

Many of the rooms were occupied, although some were empty and falling in disrepair. When the demolition crew came by, it went something like this - "What furniture do you want on the first few floors?"

(Silly me without the help of professionals, thought he was being so kind and generous!)

I made some selections and left some.

"Good, you have a problem with some of those broken-down rooms in the building? That won't have to be your problem anymore." He was quiet and earnest like in the early days.

When I signed and stepped out into the clear blue skies with my children reveling in the newfound freedom and respect of self, I had no idea what I had just left behind. Can you imagine the value of that building (estate) now?

Have you ever driven on a really bad road (outside of the US most likely) and dropped into a hidden pothole? You wince. And so does the car. It's as if the shocks in the car themselves are crying - WATCHOUT! That's how you will feel from the gut, years later if you leave without addressing the question, "What's in it for me?"

If you're a mom, "What's in it for me?" Is closely followed by "What's in it for them?" Children are the casualties of our adult problems. It is disruptive and unsettling to be uprooted and displaced and we have to safeguard their emotional as well as physical and financial future.

The obvious would be proper child support put in place and I defer to the experts in that regard. But they will also need emotional support.

There may be a need for a counselor, every child responds differently. Katy Walter is CEO of the non-profit group **Kids in the Middle a**nd who works with children and mental health from divorced families states,

"We've definitely seen an increase in separation and divorce within the pandemic," "An increase in school problems, relationship problems, mental illness, depression, anxiety all of those things we see left with out treatment can be be a problem in their adult lives."

Issues like education, holidays, and parenting will still be concerns, only in different places. It is easier for the child to play one parent against another, especially if communication isn't forthcoming between parents.

Check to see if your state offers classes in co-parenting. We didn't take it - big mistake. Old habits repeat themselves and are magnified through the lens of divorce. It's best to pledge to work together for their best good, regardless of how you may privately feel about each other. The reality is that once you have children you may be legally separated and live apart but your children will really bind you till in death you part.

I helped the children lean in towards their father and advised their father to keep close to them during those early years. I did not encourage disrespect and instilled instead a sense of gratitude when he seemed to go above and beyond for them.

Still borrow that attorney money if you have to...

Also your children are silently watching how you handle this divorce. Unless there was obvious abuse and infidelity which might make them wonder what took you so long to move on, you owe it to them to keep your "good name" and integrity intact. You are looking out for yourself and them but don't go ghetto or disgrace yourself in the process either.

Digging Deeper - Always keep good records, be organized and transparent and decide who will be the note keeper. Then make sure both parties have access to passwords and where important documents are kept and update this list or spreadsheet regularly. This helps the family firm and may one day help either of you.

Chapter 6

Are You Healthy?

Your health is your wealth

My patients come to me in the dental office for oral health care needs, such as smile makeovers, pain, and routine care, but sometimes they get a whole lot more! Because we are mind, body, and soul, what affects one area will have a chain reaction somewhere else. For example, the evidence of teeth grinding could be as a result of missing posterior teeth and teeth not designed for chewing - the front teeth - but it could also be as a result of higher than normal levels of stress.

Are you healthy? Because a divorce is a stressful event and it can manifest itself in various ways from migraines or headaches to teeth grinding and stomach problems, even joint and back pain. I know because I have been there.

I am generally very healthy. I take very few vitamin supplements and I have only had medical care pertaining to pregnancy and childbirth. But when I have more than normal stress I carry it in my muscles and I have backache or arm pain. It seems unrelated to the original cause, but I have seen a direct correlation between my pain and what I am going through in my personal life. When the stress is managed (it can't always be taken away), the pain goes away as well. At one point I had intermittent pain down my right arm that caused me to wince and hold my arm in pain for several weeks due to personal stress. I also had knee pain which I attributed to early arthritis - but nope, just stress!

We don't want to carry chronic pain in our system, because the hormone released to deal with stress - cortisol - is best designed for acute stress. The kind that allows us to react quickly and in self-defenses mode, 'the fight or flight response'. Some of the health problems related to chronic stress and cortisol include anxiety, depression, heart problems, headaches, trouble sleeping, and problems with digestion to name but a few.

Here are a few ways I have handled the stress of a divorce with its ubiquitous reach into my life - prayer and praise; exercise and movement; volunteering; good nutrition; a healthy cry if and when I really need it (gives the eyeballs a good cleaning anyway!) I have used all of these strategies to varying degrees to function for my children and to remain on the proper emotional and professional level for work.

I suspect that would be the same for you as well. It would be nice to have an extended time to relax, decompress and process after a divorce, but that is not practical for most of us. And the support needed after this stressful situation is not what most friends and family are equipped and have the patience to provide.

" Are you healthy?"

There are lots of folks depending on you to be available for them and to perform at your previous optimum before the 'event' happened.

Consider these specific tips immediately after the ink dries and when you are out on your own -

1. Create a daily time for prayer or meditation - there is peace in laying it all on Him.

2. Make a plan to eat healthy, whole foods, as much as possible, and not binge eating, highly processed or unhealthy foods, which provides you with empty calories, momentary satisfaction, and a bigger waistline.

3. Get outside! Be intentional about movement especially during the warmer months. It's hard to be sad and stressed while enjoying the free sunshine, air and moving your body in fitness or play.

4. Pick up a new hobby. I started art and I found it a calming and creative outlet when I work with paint, canvas, and rocks. Now that level of creativity has become another stream of income and a source of my own personal decorating vibe at home.

5. Find your Tribe. Find a group of like-minded individuals that you can spend quality time

with. This is essential because we have lost our primary support system, no matter how flawed it might have been, there was still the sense of shared physical and emotional space. Your new tribe might look different than you had before. After my marriage ended, I realized for a time I was in no man's land while I tried to figure out my new norm. I didn't hang out with my married friends as much and it was just my kids and myself. I challenge you to initiate the community that you don't see. You will be surprised how many gravitate towards activities and social events that you might plan because at the core we exist better together.

6. Service. It's hard to stay insular and wretched when we are helping someone less fortunate than ourselves. It is humbling and a reality check to realize that others are suffering more, that we are actually a part of the privileged. When we look at the global big picture we still have so much love to give. One of my favorite Christmas memories is not only the time I went skiing with my kids on Christmas Day, but the time I gathered a couple of other singles and read books and gave out toys and homemade meals to some of my immigrant patients. We laughed a lot that day and took them outside to play tag and soccer. Although they had ample front yard space they lived by a major road and were rarely allowed outside by themselves. That was the essence of Christmas for me that year.

7. Get professional help if you need more than the above to function at your optimum best. Sadness is normal for a time, but depression, anxiety, or the inability to function for yourself and your kids are red flags calling out for extra support. No shame or judgment.

I have been alone on the major holidays, but not lonely. I have been intentional about finding opportunities to serve or explore during that time. We are mind, body, and soul. Make sure in the immediate period following the divorce that you are mindful of staying healthy.

For you.

For your children.

For others, you may have not yet met, but who are depending on you as well.

Digging Deeper - Plan for the holidays. Don't wait for it to blindside you with painful memories or the fact that your children might not be with you. You should have activities and entertainment plans with others if you like to be sociable during this time or use it for some personal downtime after a busy year.

Chapter 7

Would you do it again?

Fear is a reaction, courage is a decision - ***Winston Churchill***

It's the million-dollar question! In my experience, the answer depends on where you are in the journey of separation. What state was your heart left in? The secular mindset will continue with a long-term relationship, but the believer is rarely satisfied with that kind of arrangement that doesn't lead to marriage. If you are older you start to wonder - where are the eligible men? You will find if you haven't already noticed that good men are hard to find because - guess what? A woman would be a fool to let a true gem back into 'single' circulation. Does a man think the same way? Or do they have buyers remorse after the fact? Whichever way it may go, women will have it hard and that is a fact if they are divorced, widowed, or single after the age of 50. So while you may be willing if you feel ready, the reality may be years of single-hood on the horizon before your soulmate appears.

Here are some interesting stats pulled from a 2021 article that referenced the United States Census Bureau entitled, "Marriage,

Divorce, Widowhood Remain Prevalent Among Older Populations"

Among men and women 60 to 69 years old, 23% had married twice and less than 10% had married three times or more. Among those ages 70 or older, 22% of men and 19% of women had married twice while 8% of men and 6% of women had married three times or more.

This is an older demographic cohort which essentially implies that remarriages have taken place at least a quarter of the time, by the time most have reached retirement age, but what about the younger divorced women in today's society?

You are hopefully wiser, healed, and ready for love because you have put the work in. Remember that grass which is greener on the neighbor's lawn and maybe the flowers and landscaping that's magazine ready? On a regular basis, someone in that household put in the work. It is tempting to look back and lament over all that has transpired negatively in our relationships, and there is a place for that. I call it self-reflection. The autopsy of the relationship, not only allows you to learn from your loss, but it helps to put closure.

Any infidelity, incompatibility, lack of growth, financial woes or abuse, or worse criminality all have to be analyzed carefully so there are no repeats with a different name and face. And then there can be healthy closure. Give yourself time. We jump into other relationships to prove to ourselves that we are worthy to be loved and that someone out there in the universe desires us. At least I might be speaking to the choir and the congregation simultaneously. As hard as it is - resist.

Get a pet. Get a hobby. Find your tribe. Talk with the elderly. Teach a skill. Find other ways to fill the void until you are truly healed and ready. And when you are ready, don't accept a man who is still raw and bruised. It's not fair to either of you.

Clear your head and your space with as much time as you need to love and pamper yourself. Review your mission statement you crafted at the end of the first chapter and refer to it often as you think of another soulmate in your life.

The pandemic, life, and physical mobility have not always brought me into contact with eligible men where I prefer to meet them - in church. I have done online dating because it's a practical way to meet a larger pool of eligible men. Has it been working for me? Yes and no. It is honing my ability to see red flags and to see who is out there and how they think as older men.

Five Questions to ask yourself before you consider dating again:

1. Why do I want to date or consider marrying again? (don't take that basic question for granted)

2. Have I autopsied the previous relationship for an understanding of its failure?

3. Is there anything I can learn about myself to be better prepared the next time around?

4. Am I healed from the stress and loss of a divorce (everyone's time frame is different)

5. Have I committed my desire to God, who has promised not to withhold any 'good thing from one who walks uprightly?'

Chapter 8

The God Who Answers Questions

I want you to focus on the God who delights in answering questions, even as He has challenged us with a few also.

Let's look at His questions and then some of His answers, as we continue to process LOVE and RELATIONSHIPS.

Question #1 - "Where are you?"

The very first question was directed to the apple of His eye when he came to fellowship with Adam and Eve. It was a rhetorical question because God knows everything, but it was a question designed for Adam to 'fess up. Adam had a golden opportunity to accept responsibility for breaking the law. He committed the first sin with Eve. But instead, he shifted the buck. And man has been shifting ever since. Laying the blame for their faults and immorality on the "woman you gave me."

Notice God asked Adam the question, although Eve was the first transgressor. Later Eve was also questioned. That indicates that the man as the head and leader in the relationship is responsible to God for the direction and integrity in the relationship. Even if there are sultry Delilahs out there, God is seeking answers from the 'priest' in the relationship.

Where are you?

Has he wandered far from God due to sin and disobedience? Was he ever in a relationship with God to know His voice and to commune with Him? This will determine as a Christian woman the quality of your relationship with God as you draw closer. If you share core foundational values or not. It all hinges on where your guy is in connection with God.

Question #2 - "Who do men say I am?"

Christ was constantly being accused and harangued by the leading church officers of the day. He made a point of addressing their hypocrisy and warning his own disciples against the "yeast of the Pharisees and Sadducees." But his own disciples took Him literally and were confused. So Christ asked a rather pointed question, "Who do you say I am?" "Not what other people think I am - John the Baptist or Elijah, but in your heart of hearts, what is your confession of me?"

The faithful woman of God wants a man who can answer that ancient question in today's times with clarity and conviction. He knows Jesus as his Lord and Savior, spends time with Him and orders his life after Him. When he exhibits the mind of Christ and models holy living, you are getting ready for a wild and wonderful relationship.

Question #3 - "What is that in your hand?"

The time had come after more than four hundred years of bondage for deliverance. Moses had been groomed for this position but was spending his time in the Wilderness School of Divinity. He had to unlearn everything the palace had taught him and then a great deal of patience. He was a reluctant leader. He had become comfortable with the sheep and shepherd life and for various reasons probably did not feel comfortable or adequate in the role that God was calling him for.

God asked another rhetorical question, "What is in your hand?" It was his staff. "Throw it on the ground," He commanded. And instantly it became a living serpent and then when Moses took it by the tail - a staff once again.

God can use anything in our hand for miracles, for His glory to multiply and be a blessing to others. It is exciting to cooperate with God and to use our gifts in service. Find a partner that understands the concept of spiritual gifts and who will allow yours to flourish and be used freely. Even better if your gifts are complementary and can be used in a joint ministry.

I once attended a youth bible study that a couple had in their house for high schoolers every Sunday evening. It was loud and noisy with the smell of pizza and much love and earnest bible seeking as well. I took my son there and looked on wistfully at the ministry I would have loved to have done myself. My gifts were not fully expressed until I was single again and made my own decisions.

You have heard it said the couple that prays together, stays together? I would agree and also add that the couple that is in ministry together, also has a strong chance of staying together.

God asks these questions because He loves us. He wants us to have an awareness of that fact. His love was so great that He sent his Son to the cross to ensure that sin did not have to separate us for eternity.

If we contemplate on a regular basis what He did for us, our love for each other will be just as sacrificial and unselfish. If we try to 1000% out-love the other what a passionate love affair awaits us!

God has answered my prayer specifically several times regarding relationships when I have prayed this prayer, "Lord, open my eyes that I might see." I want to see my significant other through your eyes - the God who sees and knows the heart. I ask for doors to be shut or to remain open as He sees fit. I pray for peace in my soul about relationships. I have even prayed that his love will go cold and his attention and affection wander if he is not the right one for me.

Looking back with hindsight's 20/20 vision, I just have to shake my head and say PTL (praise the Lord). The disappointments were a blessing in disguise. I dodged many a bullet in the minefield of love, because I dared to ask God the question only He can answer definitively -

"Is he for me?"

Chapter 9

Communication Cheat Sheets

Ten Phrases to Practice out loud with Confidence

- *What is your intention?*
- *I am uncomfortable with (fill in the blank)*
- *I would like to go home now*
- *I would like you to go home now*
- *I am sorry*
- *I love you / I appreciate you (more subtle)*
- *We need to set boundaries (intimacy)*
- *Let's agree to disagree on this one*
- *I feel uncomfortable when you speak to me with that tone / using those words*
- *What does your financial picture look like (the answer with depth varies depending on how close you've become)?*

Seven Key Questions to Remember

- *Who am I?*
- *Is he emotionally available?*
- *Does he have the three C's*
- *Is he a Macy or Marshall's shopper?*
- *What's in it for me?*
- *Am I healthy?*
- *Would I do it again?*

Five Affirmations to get you started each day

- *I am loved*
- *I am wonderfully and fearfully made*
- *I am capable of handling today's challenges*
- *I am creating an exciting new future*
- *I am healthy and I can do all things with Christ*

In the first chapter I challenged you to create your own mission statement, here's mine:

My Mission Statement

To love the Lord my God with all my heart and soul and the people he places on my life's journey; to leave a legacy of love, laughter, and faith.

Epilogue

As I get ready to host a Writing Retreat I am aware that people write for various reasons some of which may include - a passive income stream, to establish authority in an industry or because the message or story is burning inside and they have to share it with the world.

You have in your hands or on your device the story that was "burning inside". My first few drafts were sanitized versions of my experience, even this final draft is somewhat restrained, but honest enough for each of you involved in a relationship or desirous of one to get the message. The prophet stated in Hosea 4:6 "My people perish from a lack of knowledge." I lived too isolated from Godly counsel, knowledge and women who could give me honest feedback in the days when I was making life changing decisions. I will not meet most of you reading this in person, only through these pages will you hear my sister or best friend voice. Take it for what it's worth - a glimpse into my personal diary and a desire to help as many women from the pitfalls I endured.

Know and love yourself first of all. At the time of this writing I am now seven years post divorce. I have seen women from all walks of life in relationships - some happy, some not. Since this marriage fell into my 'lap' more than it was thoughtfully and prayerfully examined, I am much more mindful of future relationships. I have talked to more guys this year than all my younger years of dating. But they don't last more than a few calls or texts. I value my energy and my time and I won't be giving anyone the best second half of my life just to not be alone.

I have become an empty nester way earlier than I would have liked and this too has been a major adjustment over the last few years. The kids have come and gone. I'll always be defined as Mom but now I am a woman with a new chapter on the horizon.

I hope this short read will give you the tools to 'dig deeper' in your relationships - with self, God and your soulmate.

ABOUT THE AUTHOR

Yvette Weir is a practicing dentist and entrepreneur with several interests under her belt. They all relate to her strong sense of loving and listening to people and leadership. She has owned two general dentistry practices in the recent past and works part-time now as she expands her speaking, motivational, creativity, and entrepreneurial interests. She owns a Retreat Business under the umbrella of Wild @Heart, LLC, plans to continue writing and speaking, and can be found in e-commerce ventures as well - *wildheart21.com*

She is available for speaking engagements related to this book and on faith-based or Women's Empowerment retreats and topics.

Facebook - *@wildheartretreats*
Instagram - *@Fitveganblogger and @Audaciousretreats*